Arachnology

Book of COLORS

A Rainbow of Spiders, Scorpions, and More

AO PRESS

Jessica Lee Anderson

Paperback ISBN: 978-1-964078-38-0

To Mom and Dad, thanks for encouraging my interest in science and arachnids (including the tarantula when I was in high school). - JLA

Arachnids are often multi-colored, so have fun pointing out the variety of colors in addition to the featured colors!

Photo credits, left to right, top to bottom: Front cover: Angeli Ann Dinsay (Brown jumping spider); Interior cover: Timothy Cota (Arizona bark scorpion); Copyright page: ViniSouza128 (Red house spider); Dedication page: Bereta, AmericanWildlife; p. 4: Heather Broccard-Bell, mrfiza, Egor Kamelev; p. 5: macroart, Amateur photographer, yogesh_more; p. 6: membio, Mark Kostich, Life On White; p. 7: Wirestock, Heather Burditt, Vinisouza128; p. 8: Rudi Budianto, Roman_Gilmanov, Life On White; p. 9: Macro Photography, ANPerryman, Dragisa; p. 10: macroart, Vinicius Souza, Jawakar; p. 11: ViniSouza128, Wirestock, David Orr; p. 12: skynephoto, GlassEyeStock, Jeremy Casado; p. 13: Tanto Yensen, Bry Wark, Mathilde Receveur; p. 14: ePhotocorp (top row), skydie; p. 15: GlassEyeStock, Renee OConnor, master1305; p. 16: Denis83, Dav76, kazakovmaxim; p. 17: skydie, Uwe_Bergwitz, Charly_Morlock; p. 18: defun, Timothy Cota, Erik Karits; p. 19: Wildacad, Damir Poletti Kopesic, Life On White; p. 20: connerscott1, Ines Carrara, fusaromike; p. 21: Apurv Jadhav, Erik Karits, Wirestock; p. 22: Ken Griffiths, ViniSouza128, andhal; p. 23: macrotiff, Andrew Waugh, Ladislav Kubes; p. 24: dbstudio, Wirestock, Tracy Wesolek; p. 25: Pete Muller, Pitris, Egor Kamelev; p. 26: ePhotocorp, kevdog818, crbellette; p. 27: TommyIX, Wirestock, ePhotocorp; p. 28: Ken Griffiths, Lastovetskiy, TacioPhilip; p. 29: dennisvdw, Sergiu Rusu's Images, Michele Jackson; 30: ePhotocorp, Chrisian Edelmann, ePhotocorp; p. 31: johnaudrey, Henrik Le-Botos, jaypierstorffphoto; p. 32: Jeff Sinnock, DE1967, ViniSouza128; p. 33: xtrekx, Roman Buck, Aibek Skakov; p. 34: Michael Anderson; Back cover (Cobalt blue tarantula): praisaeng

This Book Belongs to:

_____

Arachnology is the study of spiders, scorpions, pseudoscorpions, harvestmen, camel spiders, mites, and ticks.

Ladybird spider

Black widow spider

Red

Sidewalk mite

Red daddy longlegs (harvestmen)

Arachnids are different than insects and don't have wings or antennae.

Red bug (chigger)

Red

Rust mites

Arachnids range in size from tiny mites to larger species like scorpions or tarantulas.

Ant mimic spider

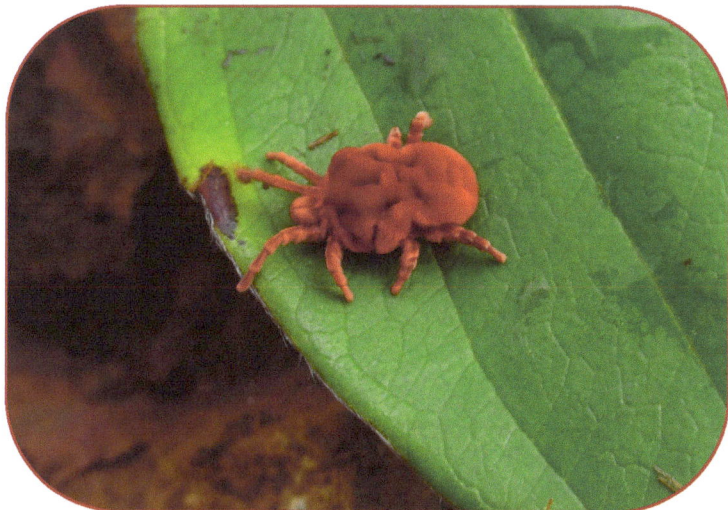
Red velvet mite

Orange

Common yellow scorpion

Crab spider

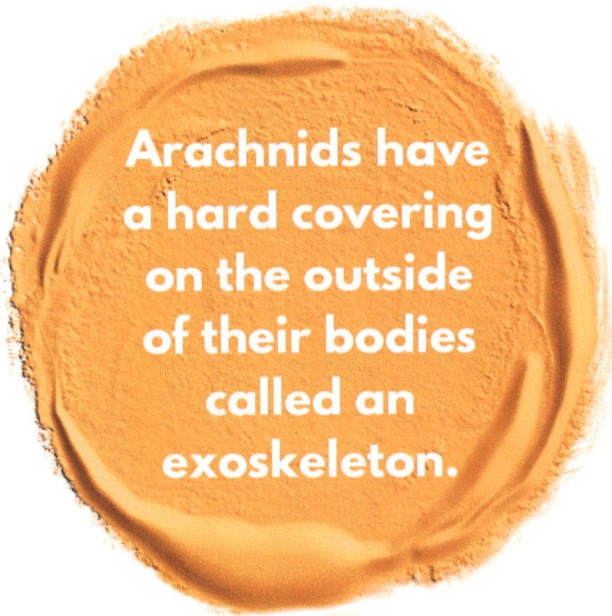

Arachnids have a hard covering on the outside of their bodies called an exoskeleton.

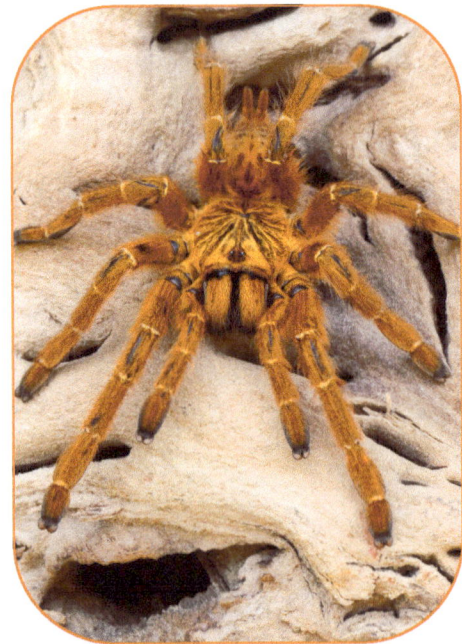

Orange baboon tarantula

Orange

European garden spider

Exoskeletons ("outside skeletons") offer arachnids protection and support.

Marbled orb weaver

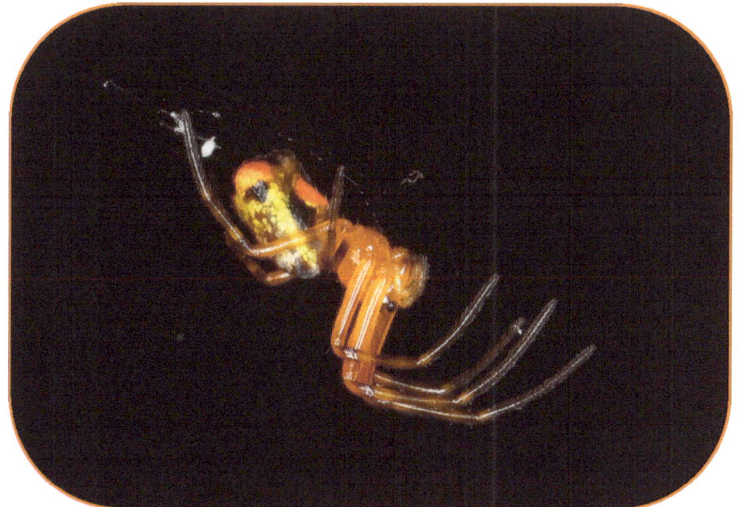

Orchard spider

Yellow

Eight-spotted crab spider

Camel spider

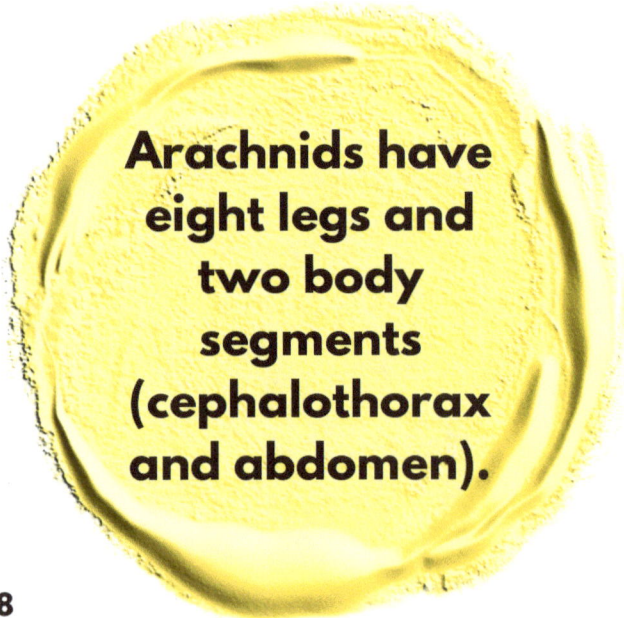

Arachnids have eight legs and two body segments (cephalothorax and abdomen).

Wasp spider

Yellow

Yellow lynx spider

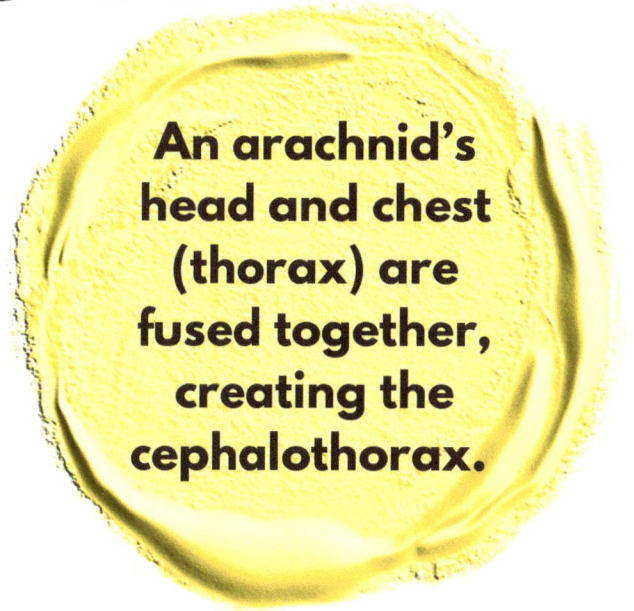

An arachnid's head and chest (thorax) are fused together, creating the cephalothorax.

Spiny orb weaver

Heather crab spider

Green

Gall mites

Green huntsman spider

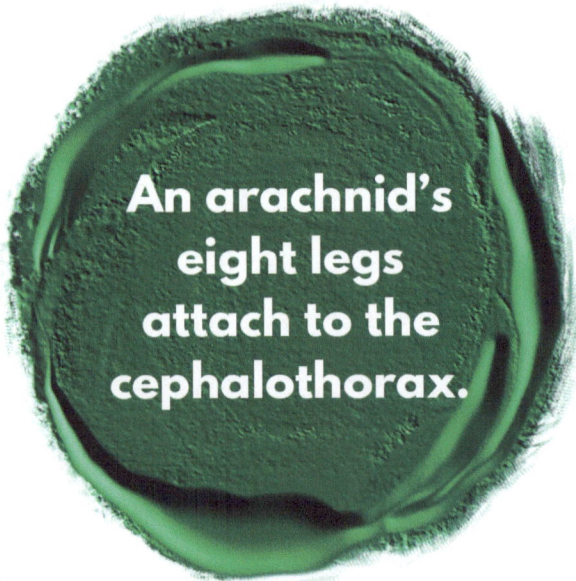

An arachnid's eight legs attach to the cephalothorax.

Green lynx spider

Green

Green jumping spider

Arachnids have jointed legs (flexible leg sections) that allow them to move.

Green crab spider

Arizona bark scorpion (under UV light)

11

Blue

There are over 100,000 arachnid species found all over the world (except for Antartica)!

Metallic blue jumper

Cobalt blue tarantula

Socotra Island blue baboon tarantula

Blue

**Asian forest scorpion
(under UV light)**

Electric blue tarantula

Antilles pinktoe tarantula

Spiders are a diverse group of arachnids and some of the most familiar.

Purple

Nomad scorpion

Tailless whip scorpion

Most spiders and scorpions have venom—a toxic secretion used for hunting and defense.

Purple pinktoe tarantula

Purple

Purivian pinktoe tarantula

Only a small percentage of arachnids are dangerous to people. Most are harmless!

Gooty sapphire tarantula

Dominican purple tarantula

Pink

Mexican fireleg tarantula

Chilean rose tarantula

While every spider produces silk, not all species create webs.

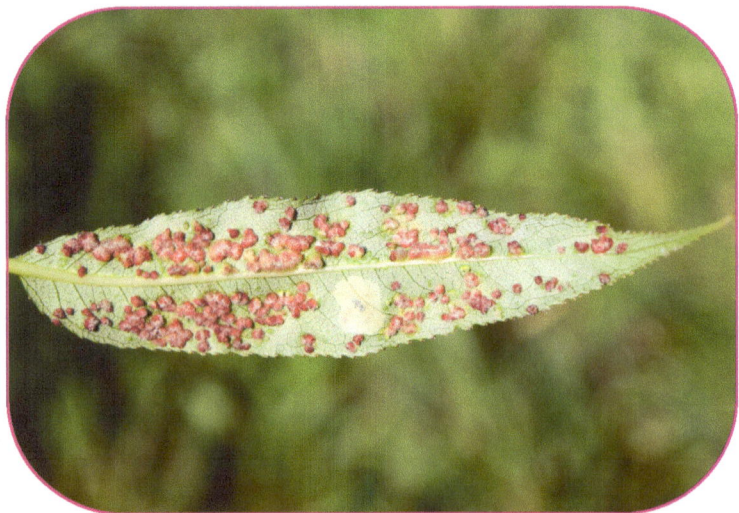

Willow gall mites

Pink

Rose hair tarantula

Spider webs provide shelter and a place to lay eggs, plus help a spider catch prey.

Brazilian pink salmon tarantula

Crab spider

Black

Ant mimic spider

Whip scorpion (vinegaroon)

Most arachnids dine on insects like mosquitos and flies. Some species feed on nectar, blood, fungi, and plants.

Sheep ticks

Black

Daddy longlegs (harvestmen)

Arachnids have special mouthparts called chelicerae. Some species have fangs or pincers they use to capture and hold prey.

Brazilian black tarantula

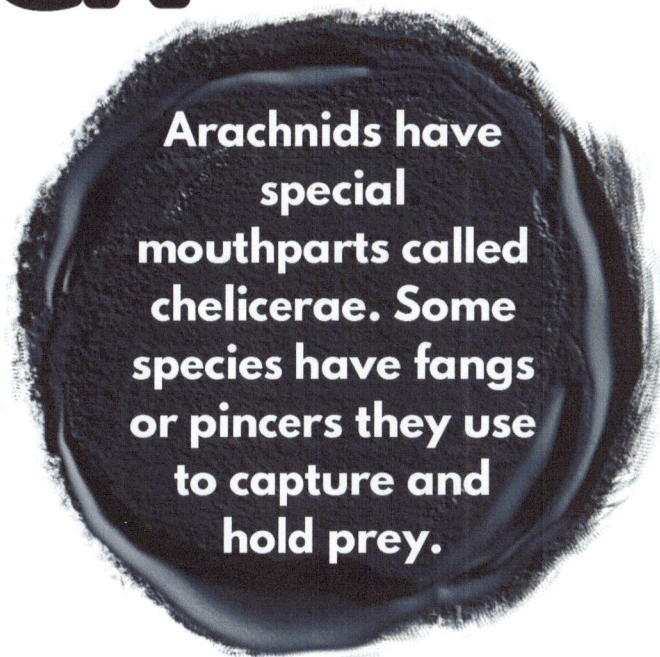

Black emperor scorpion

White

White daddy longlegs (harvestmen)

Candy-striped spider

Almost all arachnid species live on land (terrestrial), though some live in watery environments (aquatic).

Striped lynx spider

White

Running crab spider

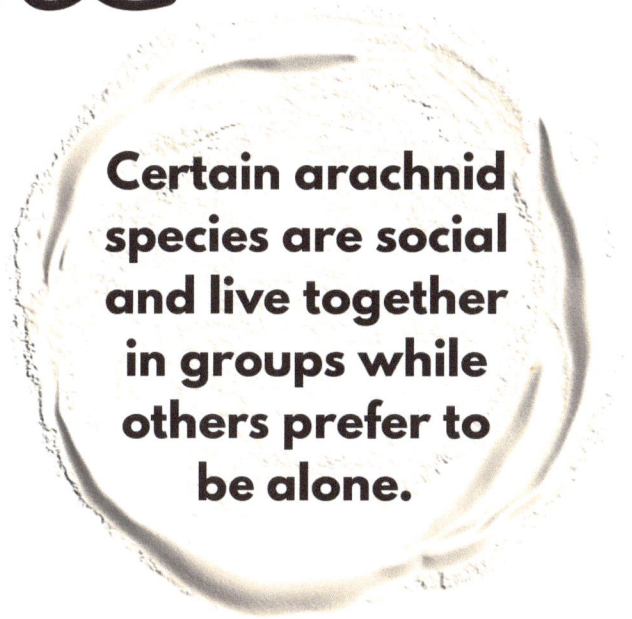

Certain arachnid species are social and live together in groups while others prefer to be alone.

Flower crab spider with ant

Dancing white lady spider

Gray

Huntsman spider

Gray wall jumping spider

A group of spiders is called a cluster or clutter, and a group of scorpions is called a bed or nest.

Cross spider

Gray

Regal jumping spider

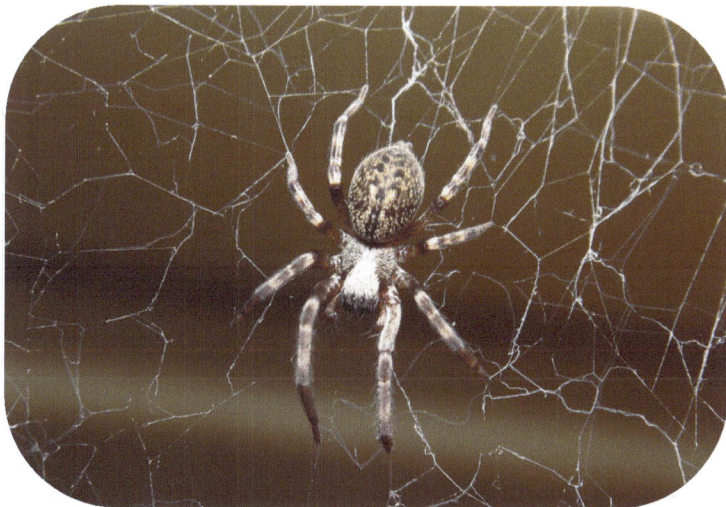

Scientists are continuing to learn more about arachnids and discover new species.

Gray house spider

Engorged deer tick

Brown

American dog tick

Common brown jumping spider

Spiders and other arachnids have inspired stories throughout the ages.

Desert tarantula

Brown

Brown recluse spider

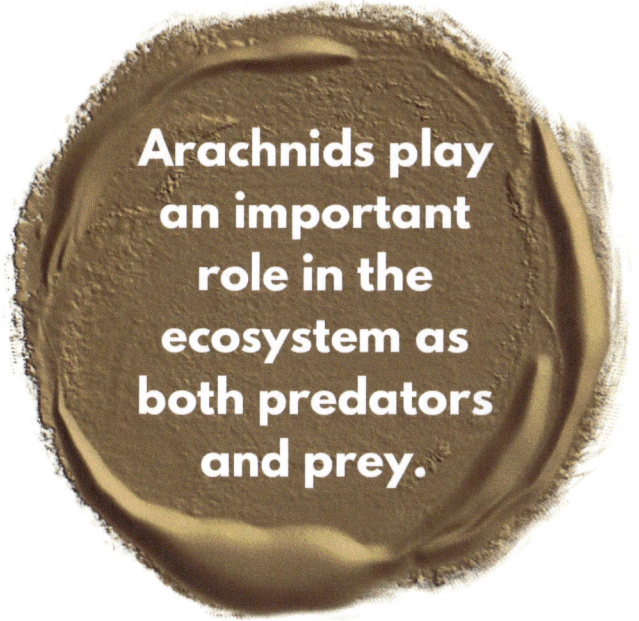

Arachnids play an important role in the ecosystem as both predators and prey.

House pseudoscorpion

Fishing spider

COLOR Combinations

Can you describe the colors and patterns of these spiders?

Elegant gold jumping spider

Bold jumping spider

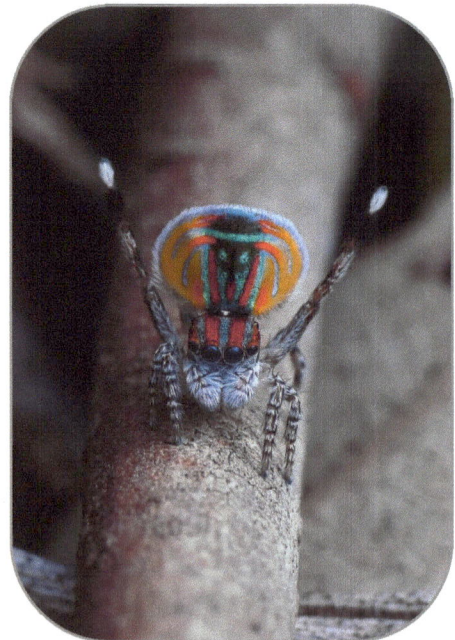

Peacock spider

COLOR Combinations

Ant mimic spider

Kipling's jumping spider

Kidney garden spider

What are some things you notice about the shapes, colors, and features of these spiders?

COLOR Combinations

What are some colors and features you notice about these venomous arachnids?

Sydney funnel web spider

Deathstalker scorpion

Brazilian wandering spider

COLOR Combinations

Long-winged kite spider

Northern jeweled spider

Blunt-spined kite spider

What are some things you notice about the shapes, colors, and features of these spiders?

COLOR Combinations

Can you describe the colors, patterns, and features of the scorpions?

Indian red scorpion

Black hairy thick-tailed scorpion

Marbled scorpion

COLOR Combinations

Banded flat rock scorpion

Fat tail scorpion

Hairy desert scorpion

What do you notice about the shapes, colors, and features of the scorpions?

COLOR Combinations

Can you describe the colors and patterns of these spiders?

Cat face garden spider

Zebra spider

Wolf spider (with babies on abdomen)

COLOR Combinations

Smith's redknee tarantula

Gooty sapphire tarantula

Greenbottle blue tarantula

Why do you think the colors, shapes, and features of a tarantula matters?

Jessica Lee Anderson is an award-winning author of over 75 books for young readers including the NAOMI NASH chapter book series for young readers. Jessica loves spending time in nature and exploring the outdoors with her husband, Michael, and their daughter, Ava! Jessica loves going admiring arachnids (especially jumping spiders) near her home in Austin, Texas. You can learn more about Jessica by visiting www.jessicaleeanderson.com.

Check out these other books:

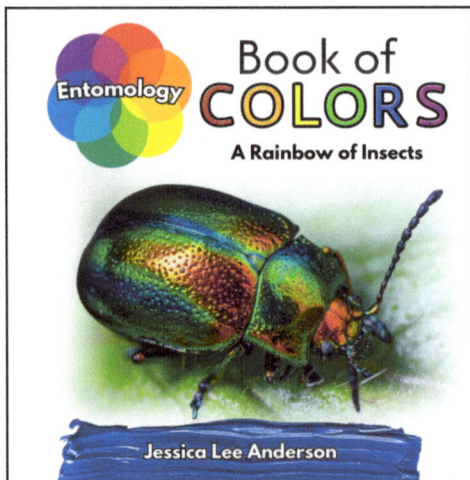

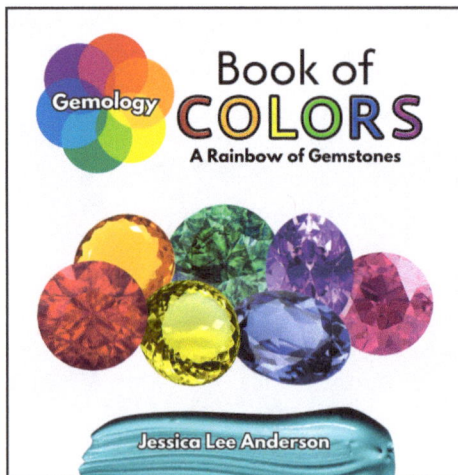

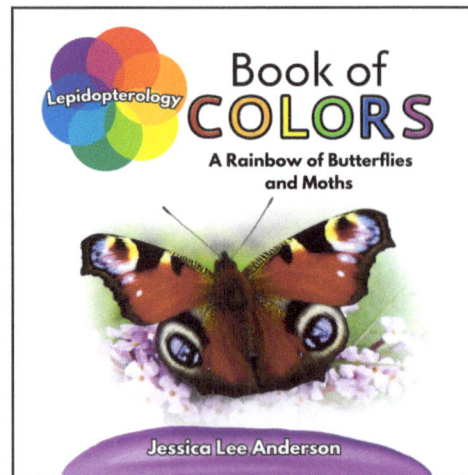

Entomology
Book of COLORS
A Rainbow of Insects
Jessica Lee Anderson

Gemology
Book of COLORS
A Rainbow of Gemstones
Jessica Lee Anderson

Lepidopterology
Book of COLORS
A Rainbow of Butterflies and Moths
Jessica Lee Anderson

www.ingramcontent.com/pod-product-compliance
Lightning Source LLC
Chambersburg PA
CBHW061144030426

42335CB00002B/93